THE
CALIFORNIA
GOLD RUSH

A HISTORY PERSPECTIVES BOOK

Marcia Amidon Lusted

Published in the United States of America
by Cherry Lake Publishing
Ann Arbor, Michigan
www.cherrylakepublishing.com

Consultants: John Putman, Associate Professor of History, San Diego State University;
Marla Conn, ReadAbility, Inc.
Editorial direction: Red Line Editorial
Book design: Sleeping Bear Press

Photo Credits: John C. H. Grabill/Library of Congress, cover (left), 8; Currier & Ives/
Library of Congress, cover (middle); Library of Congress, cover (right), 4, 18, 22;
R. H. Vance/Library of Congress, 6; Bettmann/Corbis, 11, 12, 14, 16, 27; V. Wolfenstein/
Orange County Californio families photographs, 20; Britton & Rey/Library of Congress,
24; Lawrence & Houseworth/Library of Congress, 29; N. Currier/Library of Congress, 30

Library of Congress Cataloging-in-Publication Data
Lüsted, Marcia Amidon.
  The California gold rush / Marcia Amidon Lusted.
    pages cm -- (Perspectives library)
  Includes index.
  Audience: Grades 4-6.
  ISBN 978-1-63137-615-3 (hardcover) -- ISBN 978-1-63137-660-3 (pbk.) -- ISBN
978-1-63137-705-1 (pdf ebook) -- ISBN 978-1-63137-750-1 (hosted ebook)
1. California--Gold discoveries--Juvenile literature. I. Title.
F865.L89 2014
979.4'04--dc 3
                        2014004581

Cherry Lake Publishing would like to acknowledge the work of
The Partnership for 21st Century Skills. Please visit *www.p21.org*
for more information.

Printed in the United States of America
Corporate Graphics Inc.
July 2014

TABLE OF CONTENTS

In this book, you will read about three people who experienced California's gold rush starting in 1848. Many people went to California hoping to become rich. As you'll see, the same event can look different depending on one's point of view.

1

Joseph Marks

Builder at Sutter's Mill

When I came out West, I never imagined I'd witness one of the biggest gold strikes in U.S. history. I came to California to fight the war against Mexico in 1847, but afterward I found work at Sutter's Fort. John Sutter was building a sawmill about 40 miles away from his fort, and he was desperate for strong, able men. I joined up, glad for the chance to make some money. We even had a female cook, Jennie Wimmer. There were no other women anywhere nearby. It had been a long time since we had a woman to cook good food for us!

We laid the timbers for the mill and built the undershot mill wheel. This wheel turns as water pushes paddles spaced out around the wheel. We also dug the millrace, where the river water channels under the mill to turn the wheel. James Marshall, Sutter's partner, decided to let the flow of water carve out the **tailrace**. This is where the water comes out from the wheel and goes back to the river.

I was working on the mill early on the morning of January 24, 1848. Mr. Marshall went down to the tailrace to see how deep it was getting. It was so cold that ice crusted the edges of the rocks and sparkled in the riverbed. Mr. Marshall bent over to study the sandy river bottom. He seemed curious about a gleam he saw there. Then I saw him pick something up.

▲ *James Marshall was the first person to discover gold at Sutter's Mill.*

"What is it you've got there, Mr. Marshall?" I called to him.

He called back, "I'm not sure. I thought it was **quartz**, but perhaps it's iron pyrite, or, well, it could be gold." He made his way up to several of us in the mill and opened his hand. Flakes of a yellow-colored metal sparkled in his palm. We all bent over and touched it, unable to tell what the metal was. Then Charles Bennett put one flake down on a flat rock and pounded the flake into a thin sheet with his hammer. It did not fracture or break, which made us think it was gold.

"Let me take a piece to the cabin where Jennie is making soap," Peter Wimmer said.

Jennie studied it and said, "I will throw it into my kettle with my soap mixture. If it is gold, it will

SECOND SOURCE

▶ Find another source on the discovery of gold at Sutter's Mill. Compare that information to the information in this source.

7

be gold when the soap is finished." The next morning, Jennie cut her soap into chunks. There was the gold, still as bright as it could be.

▲ *Miners used pans and other tools to find gold in streams.*

PANNING FOR GOLD

People found gold by picking it up as **nuggets** or chunks, usually as part of another rock, or they panned for gold. Gold was often found mixed in with the gravel of a river bottom. To pan for gold, miners put gravel and water in a pan and then shook it back and forth. Gold, which is heavier than gravel, settles on the bottom of the pan. The worthless gravel and other materials stay near the top. This was one of the easiest and least expensive ways to find gold.

We all wanted to go searching for gold for ourselves, but Mr. Marshall reminded us that we had come to build a mill. If we didn't build it, we would not be paid. So we looked for gold flakes and nuggets only during free moments and on Sundays.

Four days after he found the flakes, Mr. Marshall went down to the fort and told Mr. Sutter about what he had found. I'm told that the two of them tested the flakes even more. Mr. Sutter finally told Mr. Marshall, "I declare this to be gold of the finest quality."

Over the next year, word spread about the discovery of gold at Sutter's Mill. And that brought the world to California in 1849 and 1850. I was happier to have my wages for an honest day's work. The few ounces of gold that I dug out of the riverbed were just icing on the cake. I eventually made my way to San Francisco where I opened a store, but I was at Sutter's Mill when Mr. Marshall found gold and the gold rush began.

THINK ABOUT IT

▶ Determine the main point of this chapter. Pick out one piece of evidence that supports it.

Posters advertised passage aboard ships to the California gold region.

2

Charles Hayward

'49er

Every time I opened a newspaper, there was another account of someone striking it rich in California. Yet here in the state of New York, the gold rush felt very far away. At first I thought that it was a foolish quest for a man to leave his home and family and travel so far for the hope of finding gold. But the more I thought about it, the more it seemed that I should take the opportunity. On my meager salary as a schoolteacher, I could not hope to save much money beyond what was needed to take care of my family. I heard that a person could go to California and find at least $10,000 in gold, then hurry home with it. And if I dared admit it, a small part of me thirsted for the adventures offered by the overland trail and the West.

My wife, Miranda, would not hear of coming with me, not with two young children. She had also read about the gold rush and the dangerous conditions on the overland trails. I felt badly, knowing I could not possibly leave enough money for her care in my absence, so I made an arrangement with my brother. If he would watch over Miranda and the children and provide for them, I would share my gold with him upon my return.

On the May morning of my departure, I felt heavy with sorrow as I bid Miranda and the children

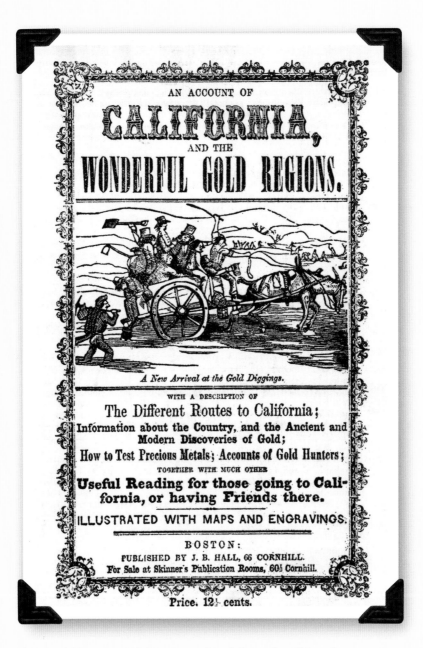

▲ Pamphlets spread the news of California's gold and explained how others could join in on the gold rush.

good-bye. I traveled with several friends who also hoped to find fortunes in California. We traveled by steamer from New York across the Great Lakes to Chicago and by canal boat down the Illinois River to Peru, Illinois. When we reached Peru, we outfitted wagons for the long journey. We were discouraged to hear that many others had set out for the West and turned back. Some simply gave up, while others became sick with **cholera**. While several of our party did die of the disease, I was fortunate not to fall ill. We passed through Indian Territory safely, and I became accustomed to Indians in our camp many nights. They offered to sell us their ponies or trade buffalo robes and deerskins for gunpowder or tobacco.

SECOND SOURCE

▶ Find another source that tells the story of a person's experience traveling to California. Compare the information here to the information in that source.

▲ *Prospectors traveled over rough and wild land to reach California.*

We traveled through the desert in Nevada, where the sides of the trail were littered with broken wagons and dead cattle. We passed endless days where the oxen plodded slowly through the dust, which choked us in clouds that rose up from their feet. Once in California, we climbed through mountain passes dark with huge pine and fir trees weighed down by snow. It seemed as though the clouds surrounded us. We made it safely down into the Sacramento Valley in late August and decided that the south fork of the Feather River was as good a place as any to begin finding our gold fortunes.

My companions and I built a snug shelter against the rainy season. Our cabin was made of

THE '49ERS

Early **emigrants** to California were called '49ers. Gold was discovered at Sutter's Mill in 1848, but most of the first people who went to California seeking gold headed west in 1849. That's why these first travelers are known as '49ers.

▲ *Many gold miners settled where they mined gold, building log cabins for their homes.*

pine logs and cedar boughs, with a sturdy wooden door and a big fireplace. As soon as January came, we braved the icy waters of the river to build a dam. It would divert the river waters away from the most likely spots for finding gold in the streambed. We spent the spring and summer of 1850 pulling gold from the stream and hoping to find a large deposit that would make us all rich. But sadly, our efforts were not worthwhile, and the yield of gold was not worth the effort.

I wrote to my brother from San Francisco that fall, telling him that I would be coming home by ship. I would sail to Panama, cross the **isthmus** through the jungle, and then board a ship home to New York. It would be faster than traveling the trails again, even though the risk of getting cholera was high on ships. I had about $500 worth of gold dust. My dream of coming home with riches to spare did not happen, but I did have the adventure of a lifetime. Unlike many, I came home alive and well. And perhaps having been away from my family and friends for so long gave me a better appreciation for them, as well as the comforts of home.

ANALYZE THIS

▶ Analyze two of the accounts of the gold rush in this book. How are they the same? How are they different?

3

Mario Fernandez

Gold Prospector

I remember the day: August 19, 1848. A ship arrived in Valparaiso, Chile, from California with a load of hides and tallow. My name is Mario Fernandez, and Valparaiso was my home until that day. As soon as the ship docked, the news spread of the gold discovered in California. It was said that a man could get rich with just a few days' work. Some people were skeptical until more ships and the newspapers confirmed the rumor. Since I had no wife or family, I decided to go to California to see if I could make my fortune. It didn't matter that I barely spoke English. There would be many of us from Chile and we would work together. My father had mined for gold in Chile, and he taught me how to do it.

As news spread, it was difficult to find a place on any ship that was going to San Francisco, California, but I was able to buy my passage on one of them. In many ways, we Chileans were lucky because we were able to get to California well before the flood of '49ers. Traveling by ship was much faster than traveling by wagon. I stepped foot on the docks of San Francisco in October 1848. The city was filthy, filled with flimsy wooden buildings crowded together on muddy streets.

▲ *San Francisco was rapidly growing in 1848 and 1849.*

As soon as I could, I left to work in the gold mines near the town of Sonora. Because I already knew how to mine for gold, I found myself teaching some of the Anglos how to dig mine

shafts or pan for gold. *Anglos* was what we called the Americans. I taught them how to dry-wash sand to find gold flakes when there was not enough water for panning. We would fill a large bowl with sand and toss the contents into the air over and over, blowing on it as it fell and catching it in the bowl again until only gold remained in the bottom. I showed them how to use a long curved knife called a *corvo* to pick gold from cracks in the rocks. I also used the hollowed-out horn of a cow, called a *poruña*, to test sand for its gold content. Some of my Chilean friends who were experienced stonecutters even cut a large stone wheel from rock. It was used to crush ore, the solid chunks of rock that contained gold, to make it easier to get the gold inside. We had hundreds of years of mining experience to use, taught to us by our fathers and their fathers before them in the mines of Chile.

▲ *Miners used different methods to mine gold in California.*

Soon Anglos were calling our settlements Chili Camps. We did not always get along well with the Americans. Chilean neighborhoods in San Francisco were robbed and damaged by the Hounds, a group of men who acted as though they were soldiers. They forced Chilean merchants to pay them protection money. When the merchants refused, the Hounds threatened them. For those of us working in the mines, the government imposed a foreign miners' tax in 1850. It required any foreign-born miner to pay $20 for a license to mine. Many believed that Americans should have the most access to California's riches. They did not like foreign miners competing with them. Sometimes we even found more gold than the Americans did. The tax was intended to drive miners from Latin America and China out of the mines. I paid the money for my license, but I was angry to be so openly **discriminated** against.

SECOND SOURCE

▶ Find another source on mining for gold. Compare the information there to the information in this source.

THINK ABOUT IT

▶ Determine the main point of this paragraph. Pick out one piece of evidence that supports it.

I worked the mines around Sonora until the gold ran out there. Then I went into the Sierra Mountains with some of my fellow Chileans. We extracted gold from quartz rock, the first miners in California who did this. By the end of 1849, many more Anglos were coming to California from the eastern United States.

Hispanics were not treated well by the Anglos though. So in 1850 I decided it was time to go home. I had indeed made my fortune, and I took a ship back to my beloved Valparaiso. There I opened a successful hotel and store and lived the rest of my days in comfort. The Americans may have looked down at those of us who came from Chile, but we had the right experience and

▲ *Chinese miners also came to California for gold and were discriminated against by Americans.*

equipment to mine gold. I am glad I went to California, but I am very glad to have come home again.

WHO GOT RICH?

Not everyone who went to California during the gold rush got rich. Thousands did make fortunes, mostly those who were there early on before the rush of people arrived in 1849 and 1850. Millions of dollars worth of gold was mined before this surface gold ran out. However, many of the people who made the most money during this time were merchants who sold goods to miners. Companies such as Levi Strauss clothing, Wells Fargo bank, and Armour Meat got their start in San Francisco during this time.

▲ *In the decades of the gold rush, businesses in San Francisco and other California towns grew and thrived.*

LOOK, LOOK AGAIN

Take a look at this cartoon, which is called "The Way They Go to California." Then answer the following questions:

1. What would a builder at Sutter's Mill think about this cartoon? What might he notice about this image?

2. What might a '49er feel about this cartoon, since he traveled to California in a wagon? What might he tell his family about this image?

3. What do you think a person who traveled by boat to California would say about this cartoon?

GLOSSARY

cholera (KAH-lur-uh) a serious disease that causes severe vomiting and diarrhea and that often results in death

discriminate (diss-KRIM-uh-nate) to treat a person or group of people unfairly

emigrant (EM-i-gruhnt) a person who leaves a country or region to live in another one

isthmus (ISS-muhss) a narrow piece of land that is between two bodies of water

nugget (NUHG-it) a small lump or chunk of something, such as a valuable metal

quartz (KWORTS) a hard mineral that comes in many forms and colors

shaft (SHAFT) a long, narrow passage that leads down into something, such as a mine

tailrace (TAYL-rayss) a water channel below a dam or water mill

LEARN MORE

Further Reading

Friedman, Mel. *The California Gold Rush.* New York: Children's Press, 2010.

Holub, Joan. *What Was the Gold Rush?* New York: Grosset & Dunlap, 2013.

Olson, Tod. *How to Get Rich in the California Gold Rush: An Adventurer's Guide to the Fabulous Riches Discovered in 1848.* Washington, D.C.: National Geographic Children's Books, 2008.

Web Sites

American Experience: The Gold Rush
http://www.pbs.org/wgbh/amex/goldrush/
This Web site has information about the history of the California gold rush.

8 Things You May Not Know About the California Gold Rush
http://www.history.com/news/8-things-you-may-not-know-about-the-california-gold-rush
This is an interesting site with lesser-known facts about the California gold rush.

INDEX

ABOUT THE AUTHOR

Marcia Amidon Lusted has written 90 books and more than 450 magazine articles for young readers. She is also an associate editor for Cobblestone Publishing's six magazines, as well as a writing instructor and a musician. She lives in New Hampshire.